A Pancho Bandito book™. Text © 2016 Michael Sundy. Illustrations © 2016 Jonathan Sundy.
Published by Legbug. www.legbug.com

For more information, email phastman@hotmail.com

No part of this book may be reproduced or transmitted in any form or by any means, electronic or mechanical, including photocopying, recording, or by any information retrieval and storage system, without written permission from the publisher.

The cover font is Cowboy Western by FontMesa.

PANCHO BANDITO
and the Avocado Desperadoes

Written by Mike Sundy

Illustrated by Jonathan Sundy

Pancho Bandito and the Amarillo Armadillo mosied back from a cattle run in California. Their reverie was disturbed by a cry for help.

This ain't fixin' to be a fair fight.

It don't concern you, giant freak. Skedaddle before I turn you into buzzard lunch.

A nervous desperado bolted with the avocadoes and Pancho gave chase. Quicker than a viper strike, El Pico drew his pistol and grazed Pancho with a bullet.

Abuelita traced a map as they ate dinner. "The legend said the Olmecs fled here from Mexico many harvests ago. They hid a great power in the mountains called *Paku*, the 'Sky Hand.'"

At dawn, Pancho and AA galloped to the mountains.

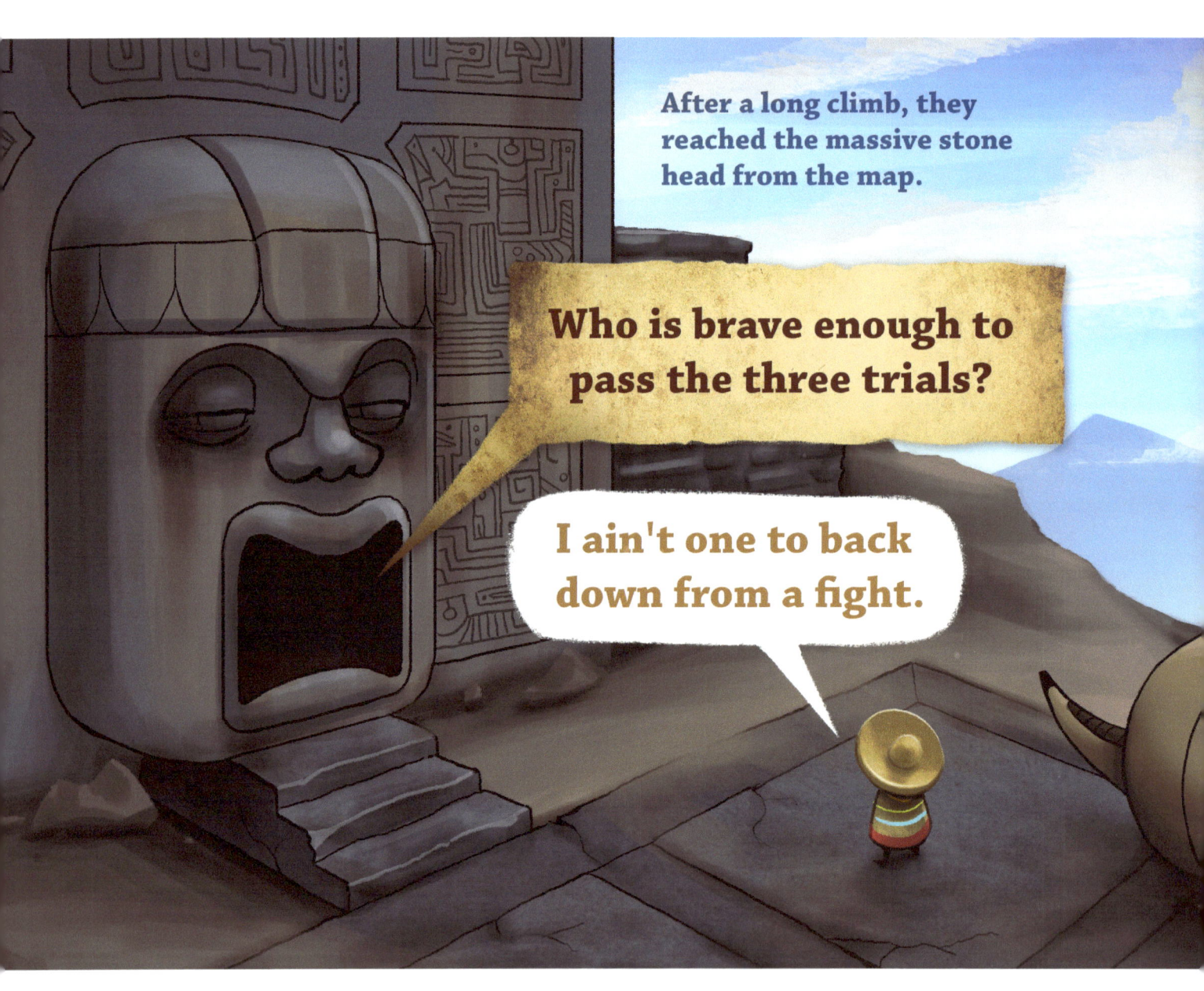

Pancho answered, "GREED."
The stone head groaned open to reveal an entrance.

The bird statue knocked AA over and took flight. Pancho said to AA, "Git me on that overgrown chicken." AA launched him - Pancho wrangled the beast into a wall and knocked it clean out. They entered the final room.

They marveled at a peculiar divided lake. Each part held different elements: water, rocks, and lava. A stone vase rested on a pedestal in the center.

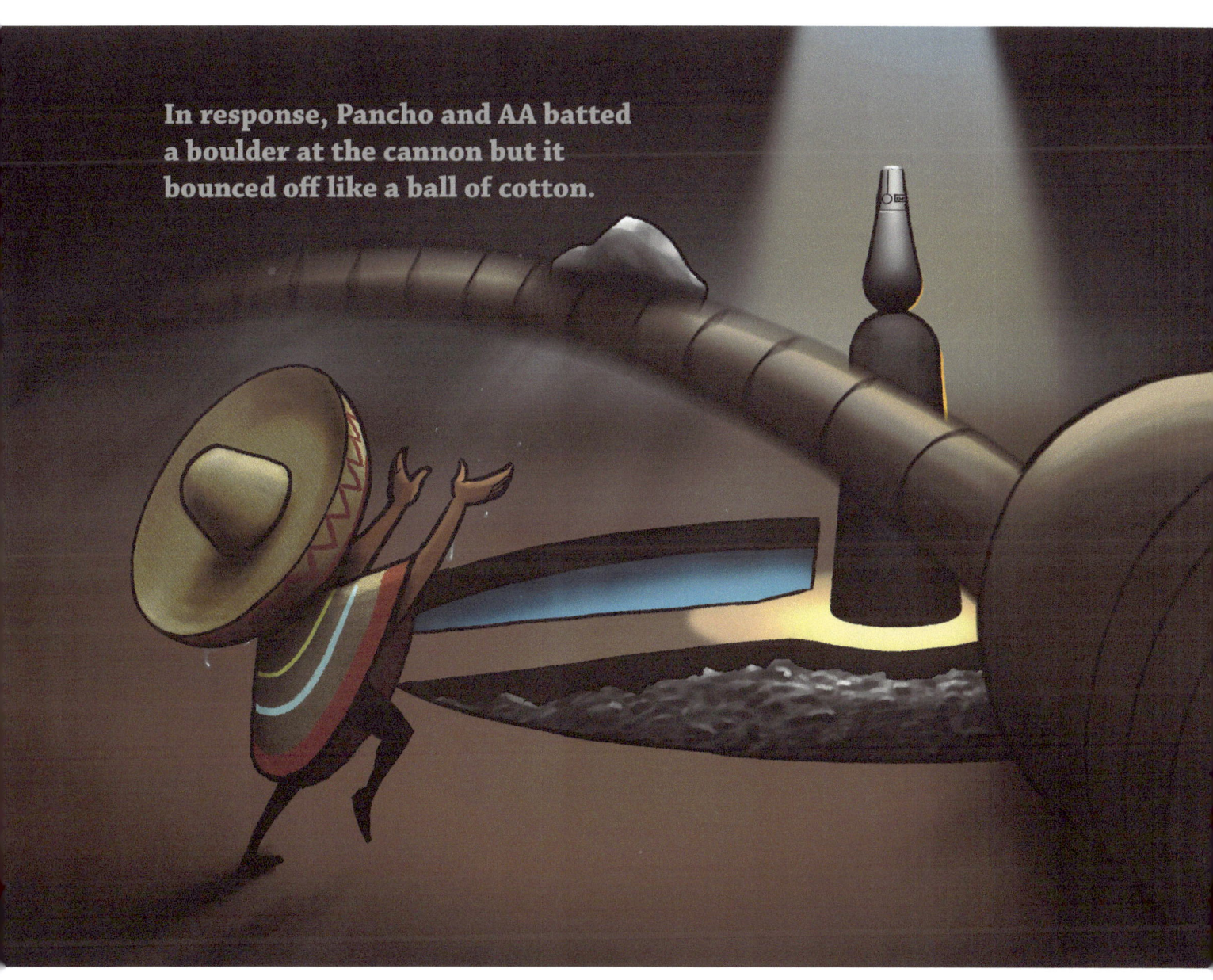

In response, Pancho and AA batted a boulder at the cannon but it bounced off like a ball of cotton.

The cannon skipped the rock pile, sucked up hot lava, and pointed full bore at them.

Pancho spied through the skylight that it was high noon! They burnt the breeze down the mountain.

Meanwhile, the desperadoes were whoopin' and hollerin' and raisin' a ruckus as terrified farmers brought in the harvest.

As Pancho rode into town, El Pico knocked Abuelita to the dirt.

Don't hold out on me, Granny. Gordito gets everything.

El Pico drew his gun. Pancho was stunned when his bracelet turned into the Sky Hand…

Pancho ducked and sucked avocadoes into the Sky Hand. He and AA picked off desperadoes till there weren't no fight left in 'em.

You and your kind are all alike, freak. Get on with it, then.

Pancho sighted down the Sky Hand at the despicable outlaw...

The farmers threw a fiesta with the best dang guacamole the heroes ever tasted. Abuelita made a special batch with their favorite ingredient, Hatch chiles.

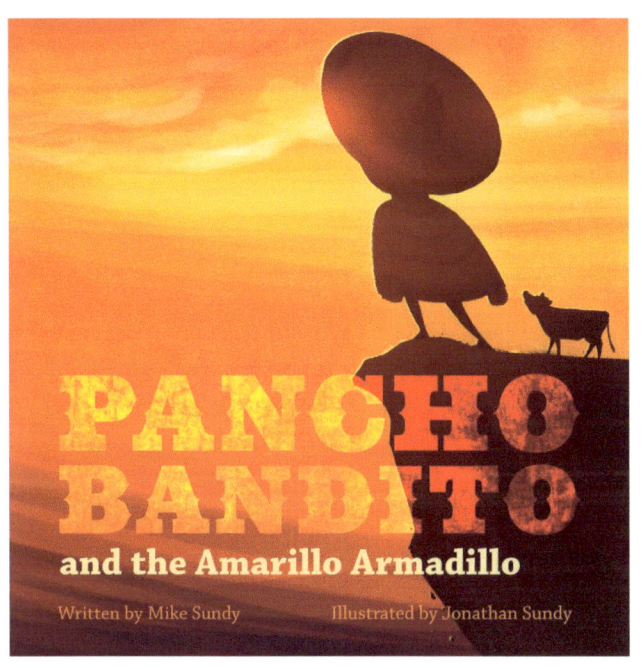 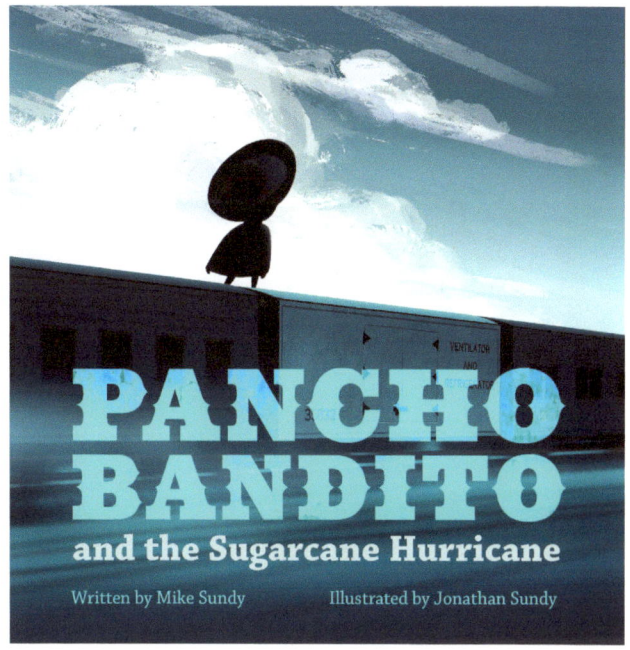

Yeehaw! Get the other books in the Pancho Bandito series at Amazon.com.

Mike Sundy
Author

Mike writes children's books and screenplays in the San Francisco Bay area. He's a Notre Dame graduate, formerly worked at Pixar, and was an ice dancing prodigy in his youth.

phastman@hotmail.com
mikesundy.blogspot.com

Jonathan Sundy
Illustrator

Jonathan is a freelance character designer and illustrator living in Bend. He attended Notre Dame and was the Design Director at Metaphase Design Group before moving to Oregon to focus on drawing silly things.

jsundy@gmail.com
jonathansundy.com

CPSIA information can be obtained
at www.ICGtesting.com
Printed in the USA
BVHW011122160223
658646BV00006B/243